LEARN BY STICKER™
Beginning Phonics

workman
•NEW YORK•

ISBN 978-1-5235-1979-8

Design by Ying Cheng and Lourdes Ubidia

The 10 low-poly images in this book are based on illustrations by Ying Cheng. Activity illustrations and line art by Lourdes Ubidia.

Concept and text by Alisha Zucker

Workman books are available at special discounts when purchased in bulk for premiums and sales promotions as well as for fundraising or educational use. Special editions or book excerpts can also be created to specification. For details, please contact special.markets@hbgusa.com.

Workman Publishing Co., Inc., a subsidiary of Hachette Book Group, Inc.
1290 Avenue of the Americas
New York, NY 10104

workman.com

WORKMAN is a registered trademark of Workman Publishing Co., Inc.,
a subsidiary of Hachette Book Group, Inc.
LEARN BY STICKER is a trademark of Workman Publishing Co., Inc.,
a subsidiary of Hachette Book Group, Inc.

Distributed in the United Kingdom by Hachette Book Group, UK, Carmelite House, 50 Victoria Embankment, London EC4Y 0DZ.
Distributed in Europe by Hachette Livre, 58 rue Jean Bleuzen, 92 178 Vanves Cedex, France.

Printed in China on responsibly sourced paper.

First printing June 2023

10 9 8 7 6 5 4 3 2 1

HOW TO
LEARN BY STICKER™

1. PICK YOUR IMAGE.
Sticker maps for each friendly monster are in the front of the book. Which monster do you want to sticker first? It's up to you!

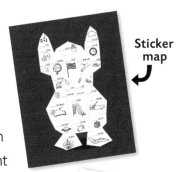

Sticker map

2. FIND YOUR STICKERS.
Sticker sheets for each picture are in the back of the book. Use the image in the top right corner of each sticker sheet to find the one that matches the picture. Both the sticker map and sticker sheet can be torn out of the book, so you don't have to flip back and forth between them.

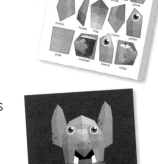

Sticker sheet

3. READ THE WORDS!
Fill in the missing letters to complete each word inside the picture. Say the word aloud. Then find the completed word on the sticker sheet. Each sticker matches only one space on the sticker map. Place each sticker in the matching space on the sticker map. Be careful! The stickers aren't removable.

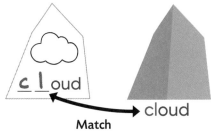

c l oud

Match → cloud

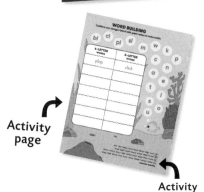

Finished picture

4. TURN THE PAGE.
There are fun activities on the back of each picture to get extra practice and strengthen your phonics skills.

Activity page

Activity Answers

LET'S SOLVE AND STICKER!

Directions

Beginning Sounds
Fill in the blanks using consonants (letters that aren't vowels) to complete the words.

L-blends
Fill in the blanks with *bl*, *cl*, *fl*, *gl*, *pl*, or *sl* to complete the words.

Short Vowels: *a, i, o*
Fill in the blanks with the short vowels *a*, *i*, or *o* to complete the words.

R-blends
Fill in the blanks with *br*, *cr*, *dr*, *fr*, *pr*, or *tr* to complete the words.

Short Vowels: *e, u*
Fill in the blanks with the short vowels *e* or *u* to complete the words.

Final Blends
Fill in the blanks with *mp*, *nt*, *sh*, or *st* to complete the words.

Beginning Digraphs
Fill in the blanks with *ch*, *sh*, *th*, or *wh* to complete the words.

More Final Blends
Fill in the blanks with *nd*, *ng*, or *nk* to complete the words.

S-blends
Fill in the blanks with *sk*, *sm*, *sn*, *sp*, *sq*, *st*, or *sw* to complete the words.

Long Vowels
Fill in the blanks with combinations of the vowels *a*, *e*, *i*, *o*, *u*, and the letter *y*. (Some words will need the silent *e* to complete them.)

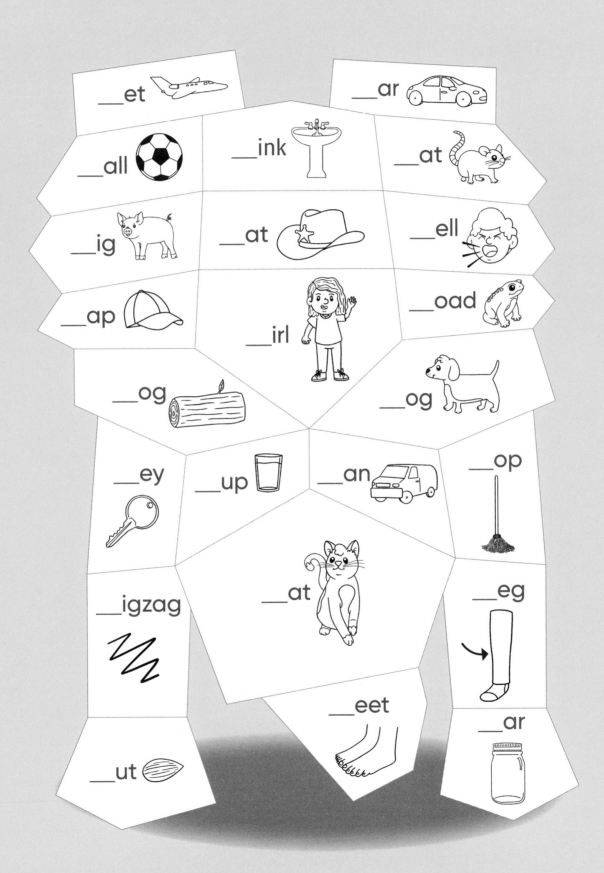

SECRET MESSAGE

Say the name of each picture.
Circle the beginning sound for each word.
Then fill in the letters to answer the riddle!

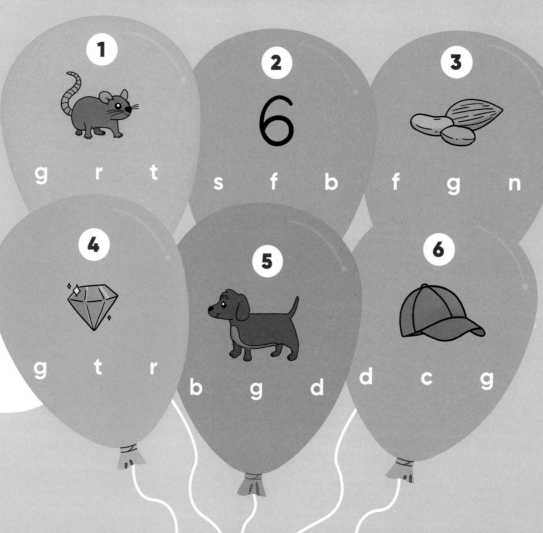

1. g r t

2. s f b

3. f g n

4. g t r

5. b g d

6. d c g

What do little monsters like to ride at the amusement park?

The __ __ a __ y - __ o - __ ou __ __ !
    2 6   1   4   1   3 5

The scary-go-round!

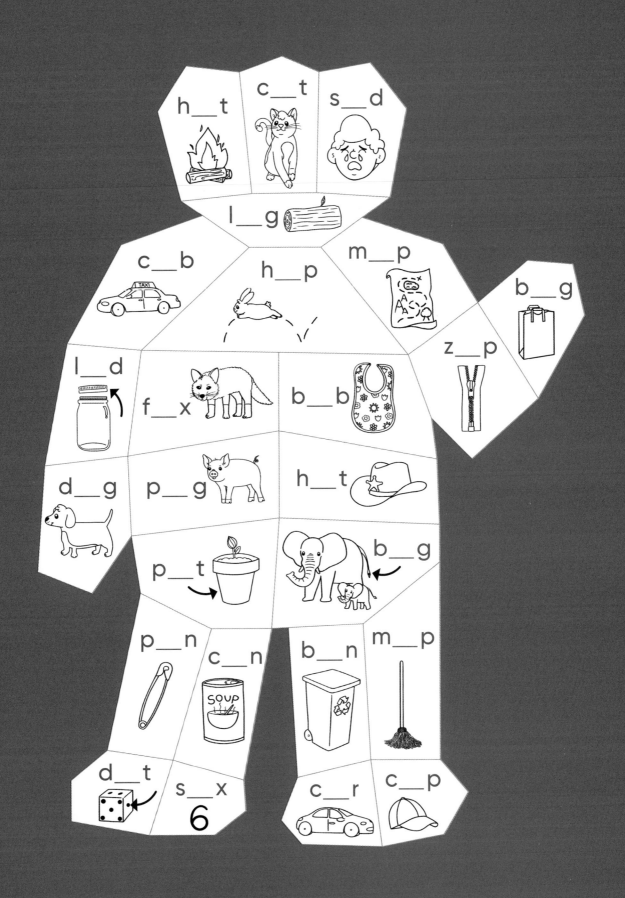

MYSTERY WORDS

Use the clues on the treasure maps
to find each mystery word.

✘ I rhyme with *cat*.

✘ I start with *b*.

✘ You'll find me at a baseball game.

I am a _____

✘ I have six legs.

✘ My middle vowel is a short *u*.

✘ I am another word for *insect*.

I am a _____

✘ I am a drawing that tells you about a place.

✘ I start with *m*.

✘ I rhyme with *lap*.

I am a _____

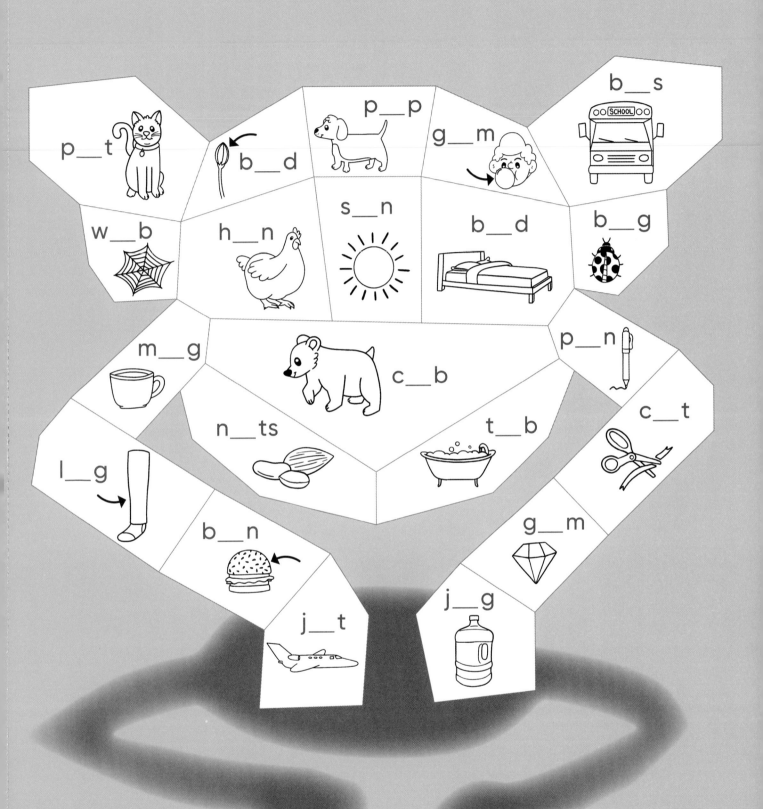

RHYME TIME

Write three words that rhyme with the word in each box.

mug

1. _____ 2. _____ 3. _____

 **jet**

1. _____ 2. _____ 3. _____

pen

1. _____ 2. _____ 3. _____

 **bed**

1. _____ 2. _____ 3. _____

Possible answers:
bug, hug, jug, plug, rug, slug, snug
bet, get, jet, met, net, pet, set, vet, wet
den, hen, men, ten, then, when
bread, fed, head, led, red, sled, wed

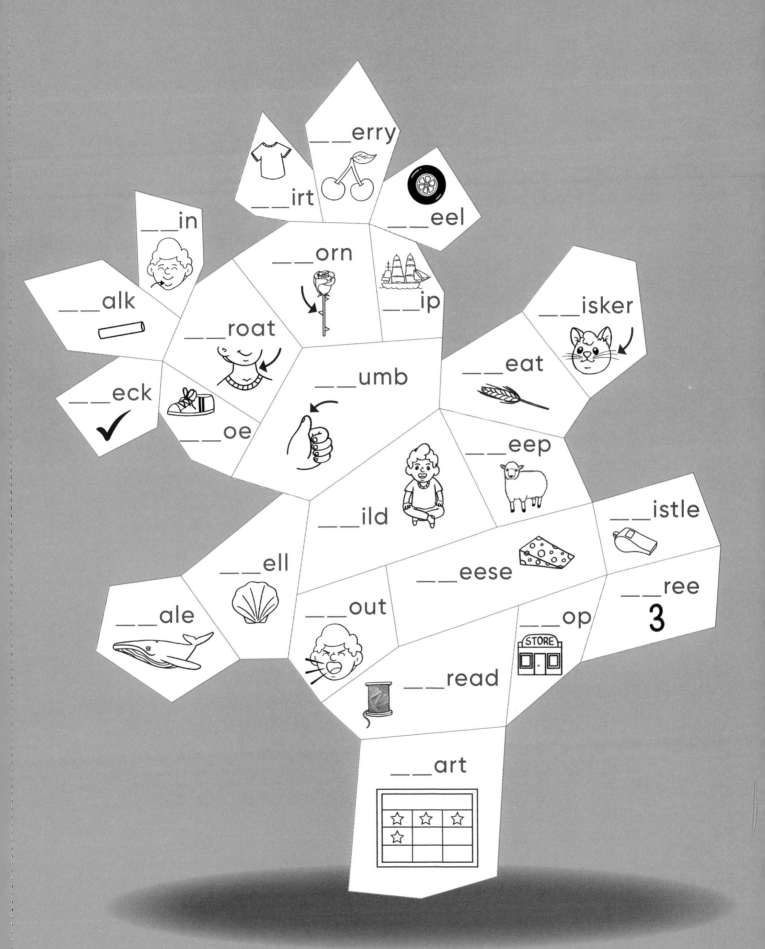

___erry

___irt

___eel

___in

___orn

___alk

___ip

___roat

___isker

___eck ✔

___umb

___eat

___oe

___eep

___istle

___ild

___ell

___eese

___ree
3

___ale

___out

___op

___read

___art

☆ ☆ ☆
☆

MATCHING DIGRAPHS

Fill in the missing beginning letters for each picture.
Then draw a line to match the pictures that begin with the same digraph.

__ __est   __ __umb   __ __irt   __ __istle

   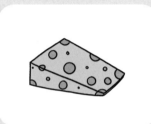

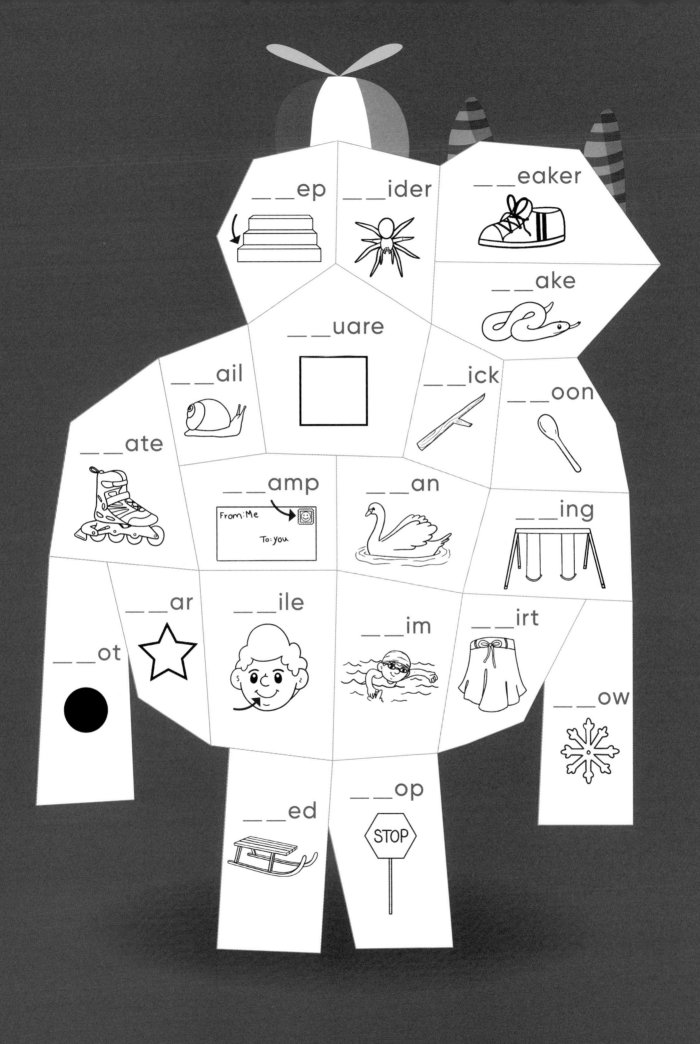

WORD SCRAMBLE

Each word begins with an s-blend.
Unscramble the word and draw a line to the matching picture.

t s n g i

_____

k n k u s

_____

s r i p g n

_____

e m s l i

_____

s r t n o g

_____

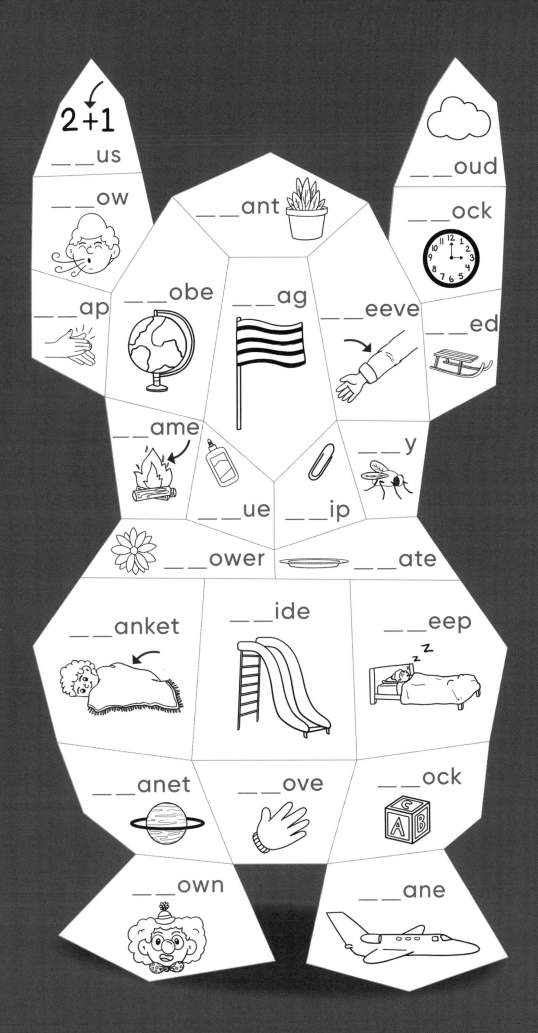

WORD BUILDING

Combine one orange l-blend with green letters to make words.

bl cl pl sl m w k p c n a e t i s u o

4-LETTER WORDS	5-LETTER WORDS
plop	click

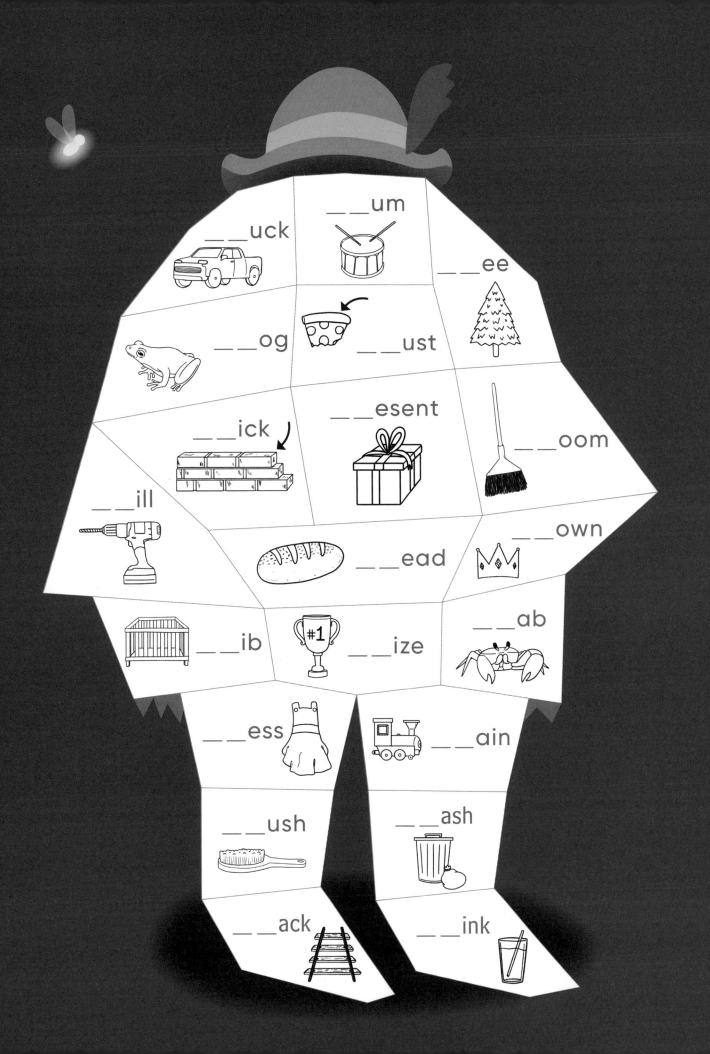

MYSTERY WORDS

Use the clues on the treasure maps
to find each mystery word.

✗ I can breathe fire.

✗ I rhyme with *wagon*.

✗ I start with *dr*.

I am a _____

✗ I am a type of bird.

✗ I am all black.

✗ I start with *cr*.

I am a _____

✗ You can walk and drive over me.

✗ I rhyme with *fridge*.

✗ I start with *br*.

I am a _____

SECRET MESSAGE

Choose the letter that completes each word.
Then use the letters to find the answer to the joke.

1 pa___nt

e   i   o

2 tras___

h   t   g

3 c___ust

l   h   r

4 ___ish

d   w   h

5 ___tamp

n   g   s

6 n___st

u   e   a

What's a monster's favorite game?

___ ___ ___ ___ an ___   ___ ___ ___ ___ ___ ___ k !
2 1 4 6   4   5 2 3 1 6

Hide and shriek!

RHYME TIME 🕐

Write three words that rhyme with the word in each box.

pink

1. _____ 2. _____ 3. _____

band

1. _____ 2. _____ 3. _____

swing

1. _____ 2. _____ 3. _____

skunk

1. _____ 2. _____ 3. _____

Possible answers:
blink, clink, link, rink, sink, stink, think, wink, zinc
bland, brand, hand, land, sand, stand, strand, tanned
bring, king, ring, sing, sting, string, thing, wing
bunk, chunk, dunk, junk, shrunk, stunk, trunk

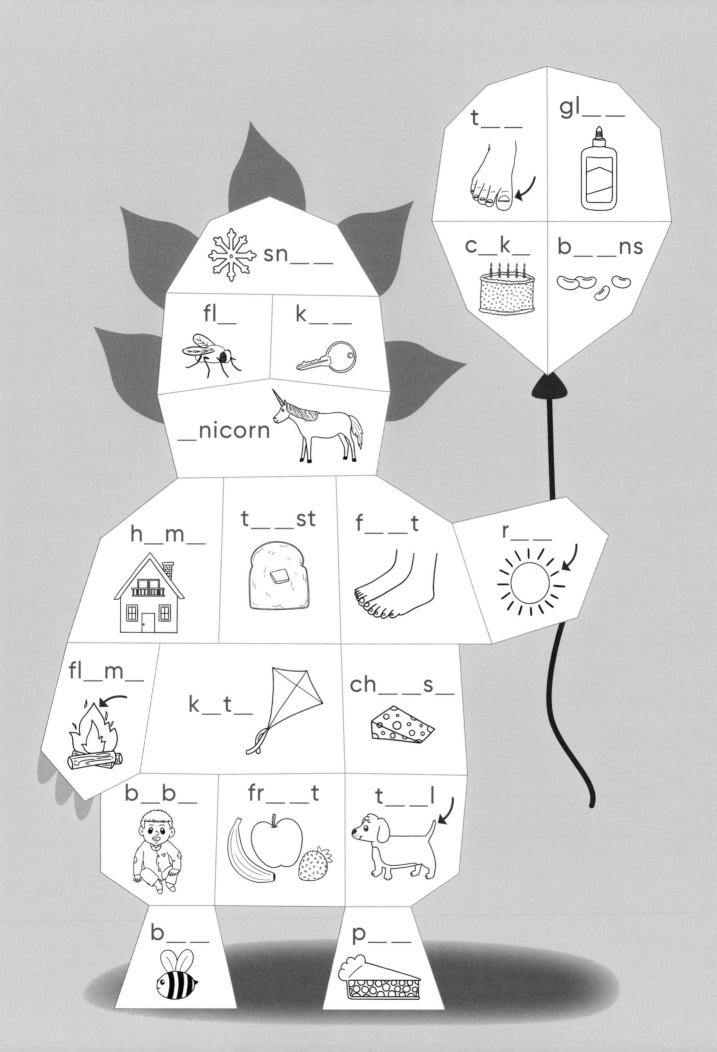

WORD SCRAMBLE

Unscramble each word.
Then draw a line to the matching picture.

n e a k s

_____

m o b o r

_____

e p l e s

_____

l w o b

_____

t a n i p

_____

snake, broom, sleep, blow, paint

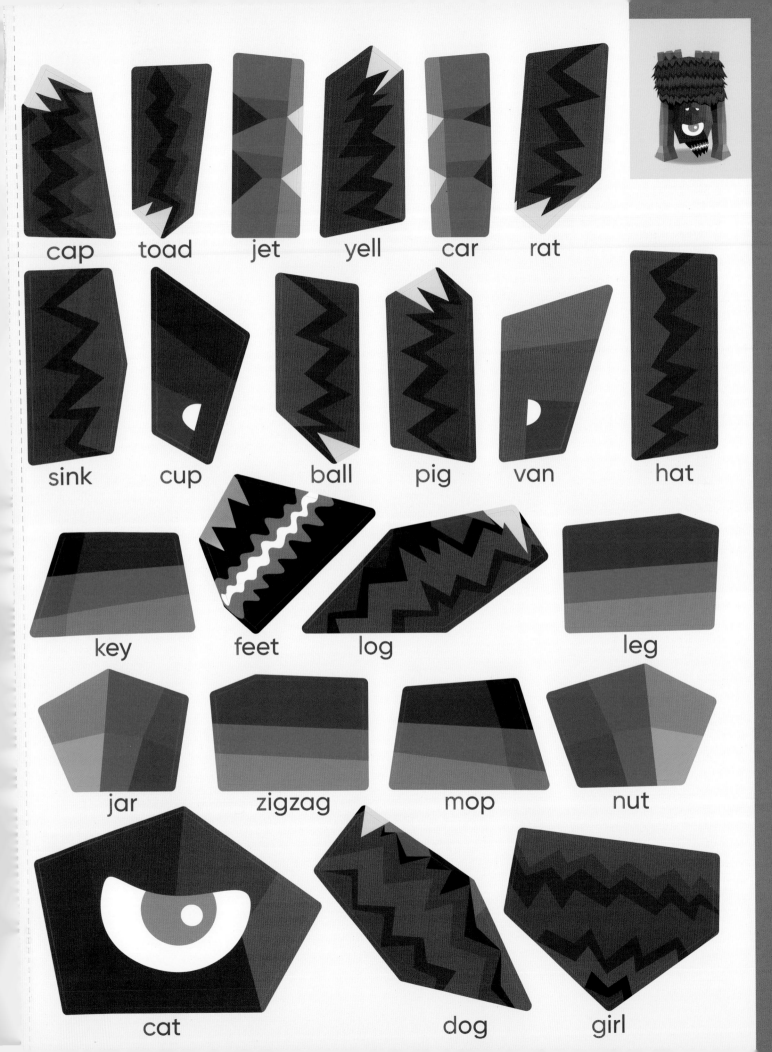

cap   toad   jet   yell   car   rat

sink   cup   ball   pig   van   hat

key   feet   log   leg

jar   zigzag   mop   nut

cat   dog   girl

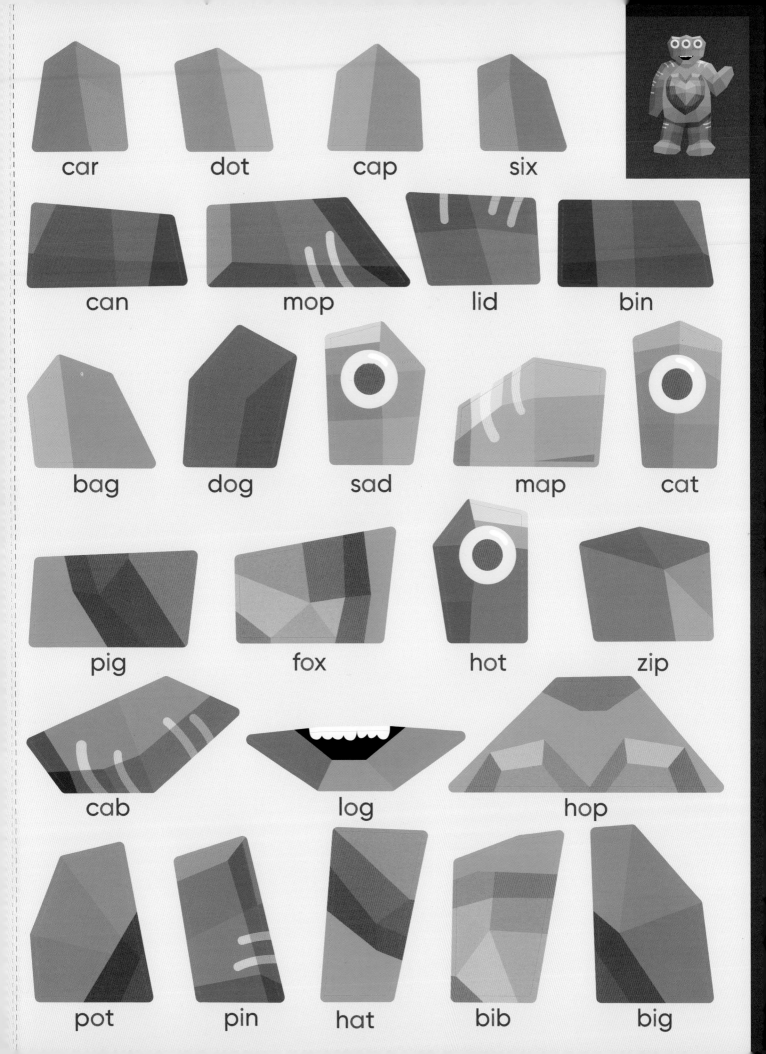

car

dot

cap

six

can

mop

lid

bin

bag

dog

sad

map

cat

pig

fox

hot

zip

cab

log

hop

pot

pin

hat

bib

big

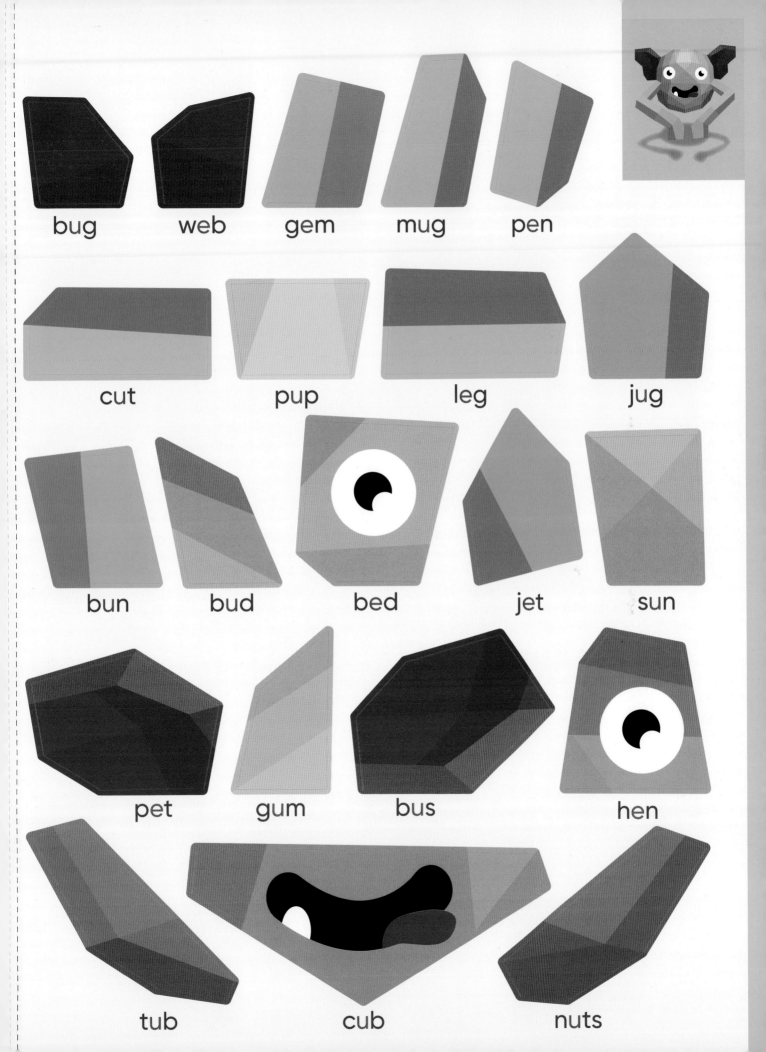

bug

web

gem

mug

pen

cut

pup

leg

jug

bun

bud

bed

jet

sun

pet

gum

bus

hen

tub

cub

nuts

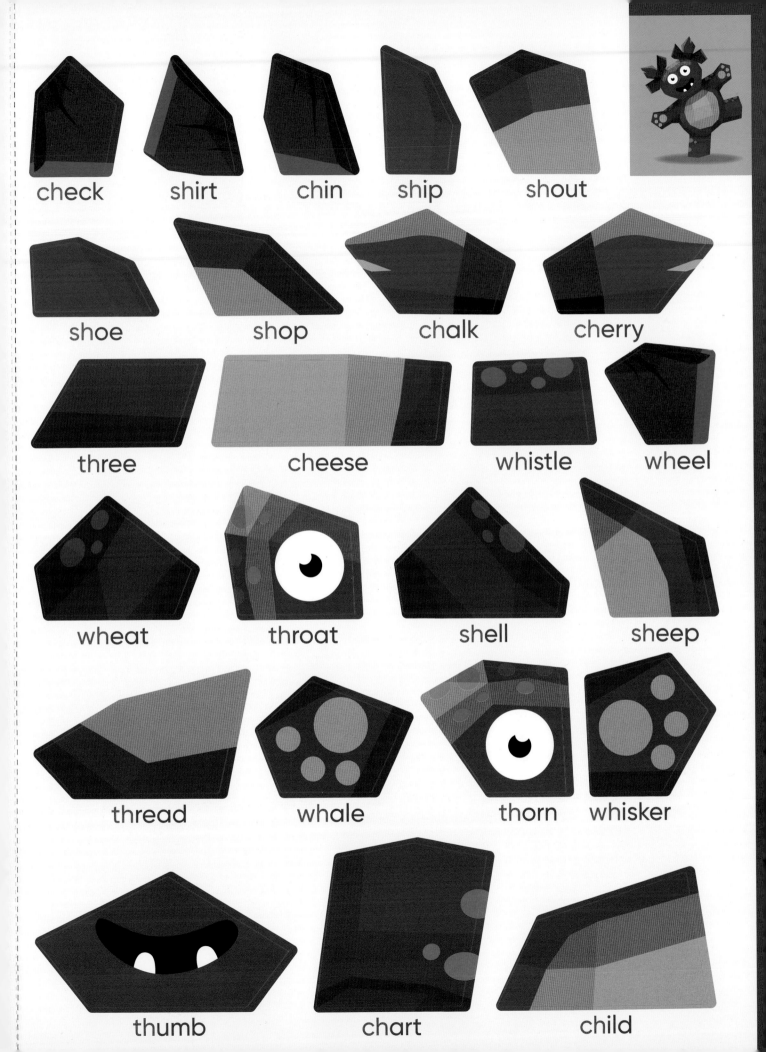

check

shirt

chin

ship

shout

shoe

shop

chalk

cherry

three

cheese

whistle

wheel

wheat

throat

shell

sheep

thread

whale

thorn

whisker

thumb

chart

child

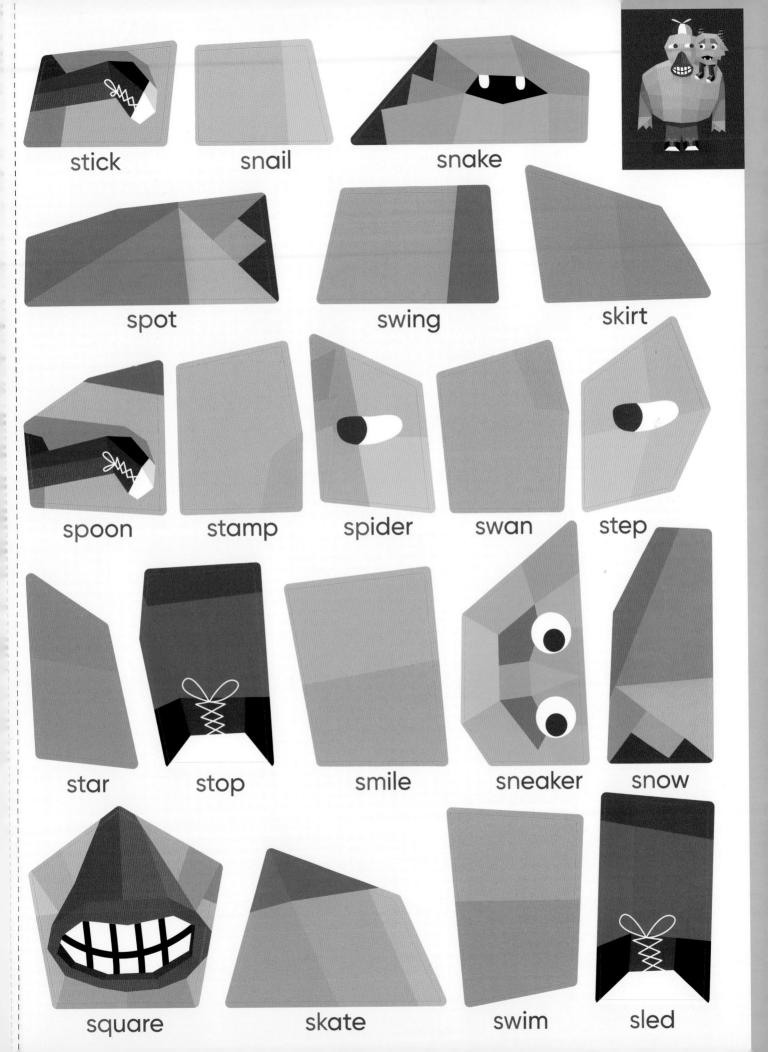

stick

snail

snake

spot

swing

skirt

spoon

stamp

spider

swan

step

star

stop

smile

sneaker

snow

square

skate

swim

sled

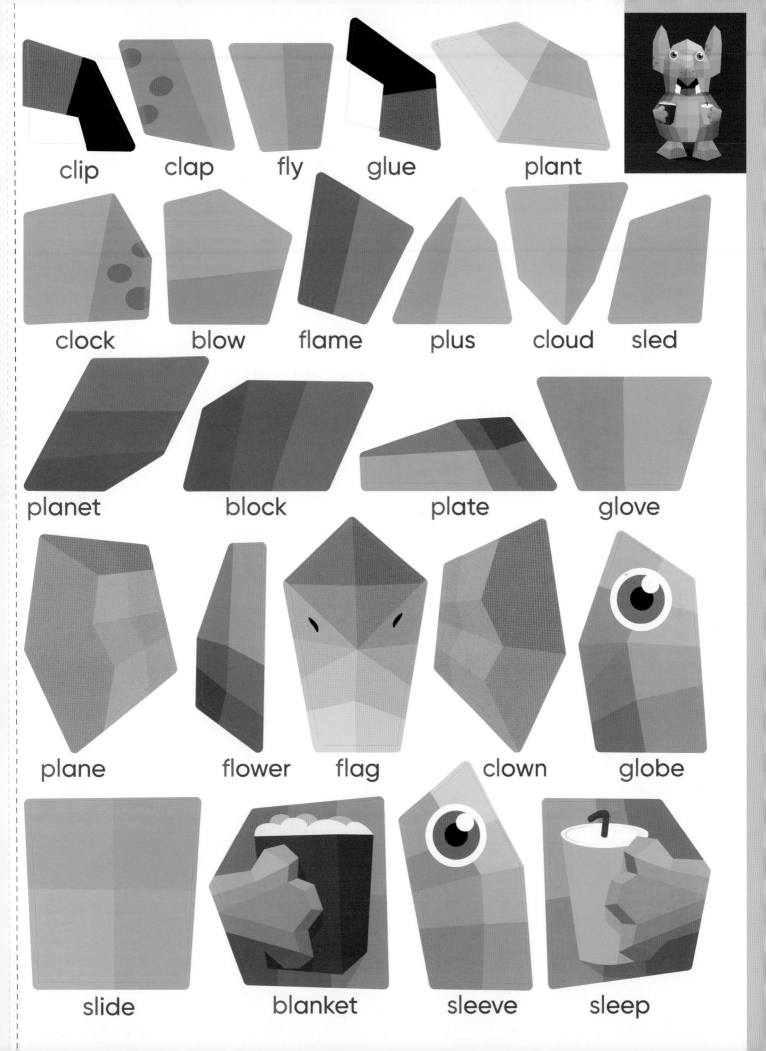

clip

clap

fly

glue

plant

clock

blow

flame

plus

cloud

sled

planet

block

plate

glove

plane

flower

flag

clown

globe

slide

blanket

sleeve

sleep

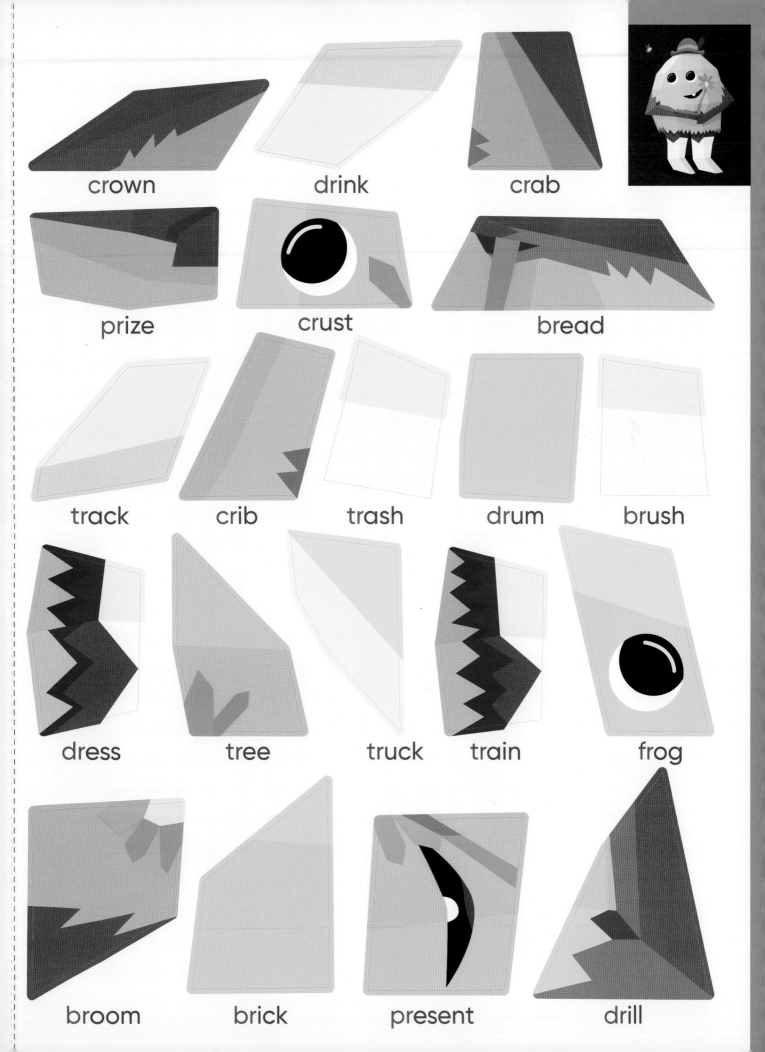

crown

drink

crab

prize

crust

bread

track

crib

trash

drum

brush

dress

tree

truck

train

frog

broom

brick

present

drill

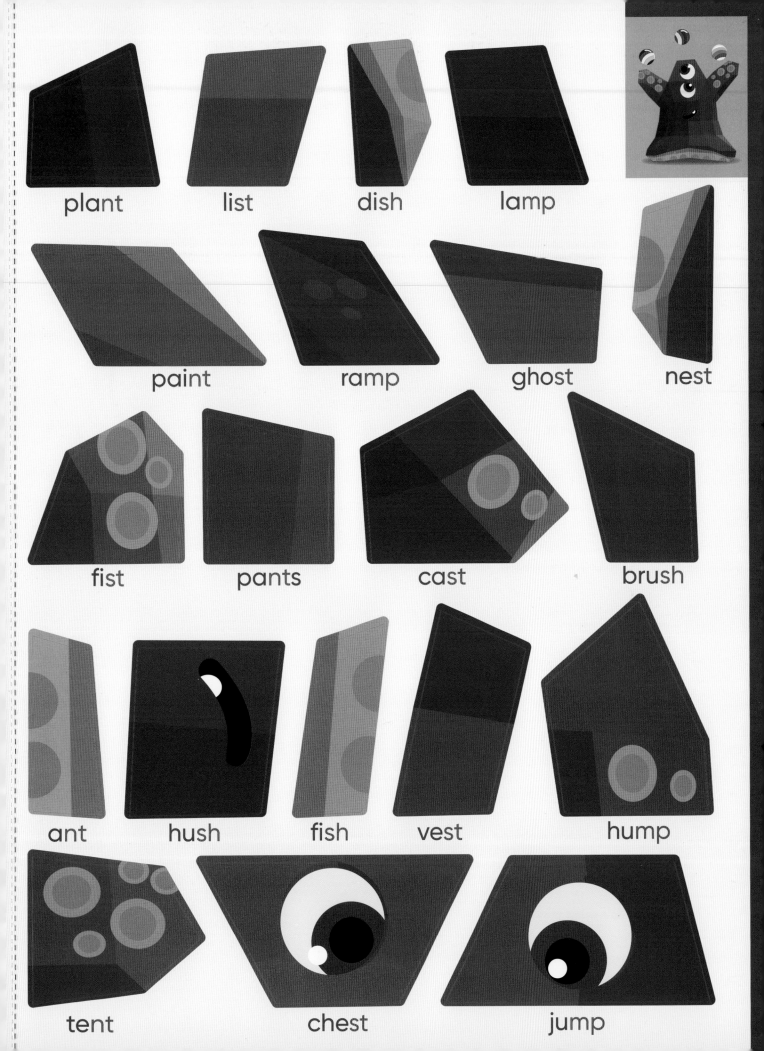

plant

list

dish

lamp

paint

ramp

ghost

nest

fist

pants

cast

brush

ant

hush

fish

vest

hump

tent

chest

jump

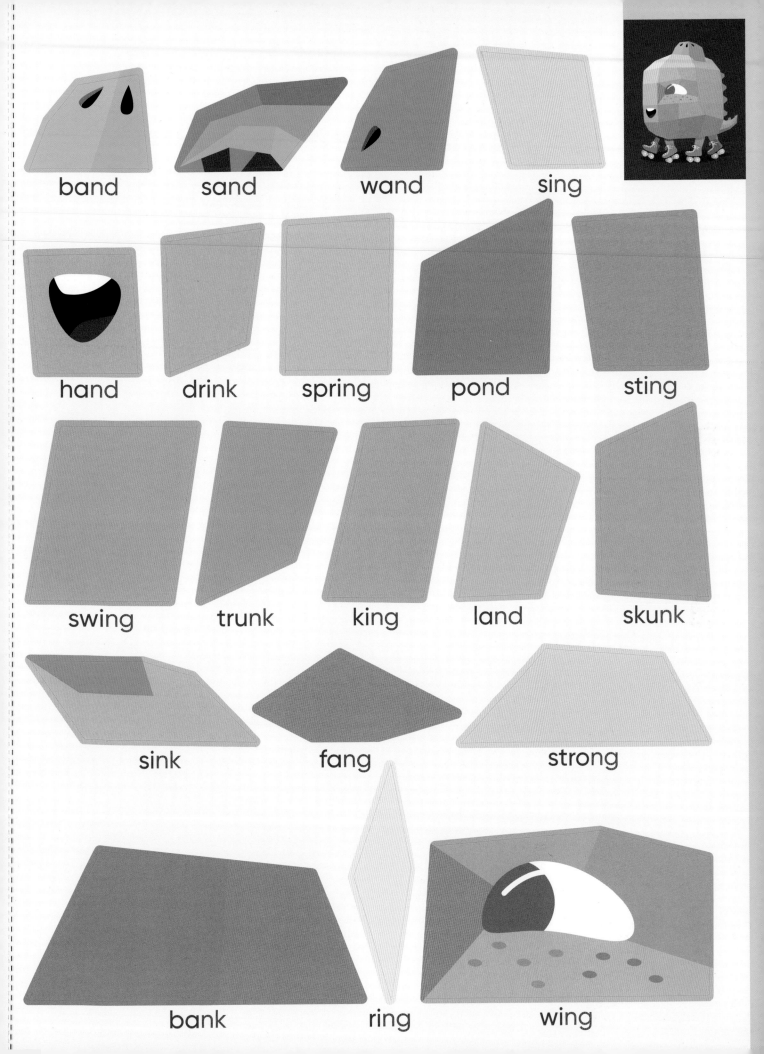

band   sand   wand   sing

hand   drink   spring   pond   sting

swing   trunk   king   land   skunk

sink   fang   strong

bank   ring   wing

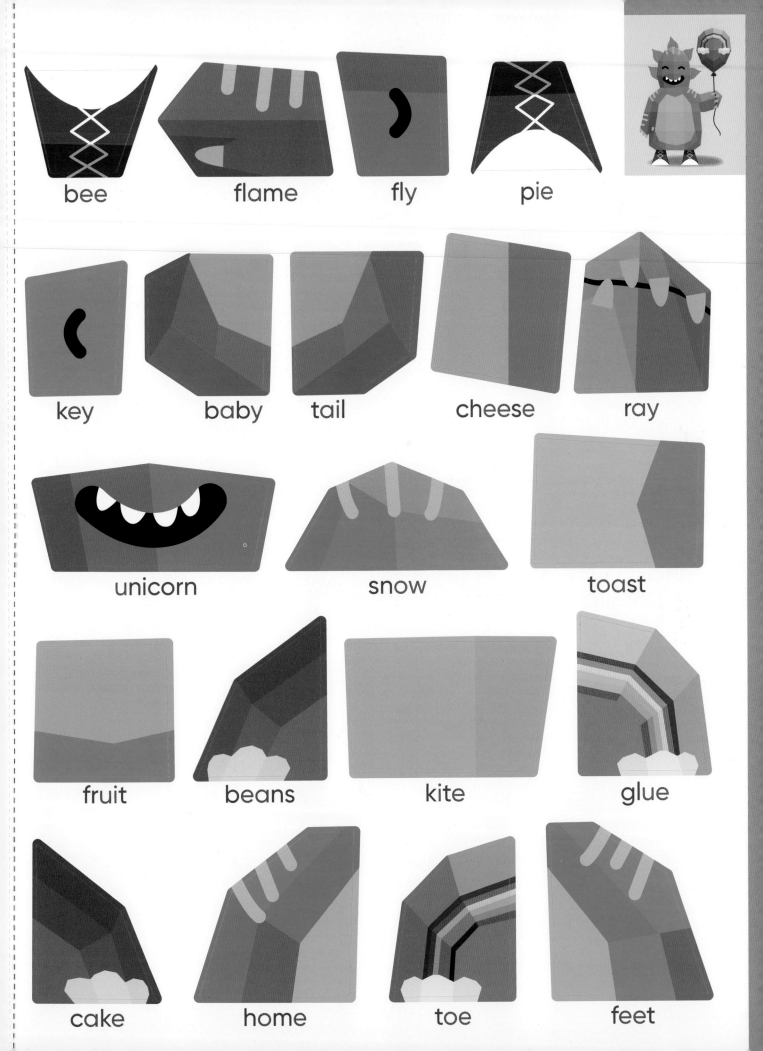

bee

flame

fly

pie

key

baby

tail

cheese

ray

unicorn

snow

toast

fruit

beans

kite

glue

cake

home

toe

feet